Original title:
Serenades of Smiles and Sorrows

Copyright © 2024 Creative Arts Management OÜ

Author: Rory Fitzgerald
ISBN HARDBACK: 978-9916-90-716-0
ISBN PAPERBACK: 978-9916-90-717-7

Remnants of Joy in the Twilight

In the hush of evening's grace,
Whispers dance in soft embrace,
Flickers of a fading light,
Hold the echoes of delight.

Shadows stretch and softly sway,
Telling tales of light's ballet,
Stars appear to play their part,
Illuminating every heart.

Memories like fireflies gleam,
Filling twilight with a dream,
Every sigh, a gentle tune,
Mapping joy beneath the moon.

Though the day begins to fade,
In our hearts, the warmth portrayed,
Remnants linger, sweet and shy,
In the twilight, joy won't die.

The Duality of Whispered Wishes

In shadows soft, desires flow,
A gentle touch, a subtle glow.
Faint echoes hum the dreams we share,
While silence wraps the weight of care.

Two paths converge, a choice to make,
Illusions dance, hearts start to break.
In whispered hopes, both joy and pain,
A fragile thread through joy and strain.

Songs of Delight and Dismay

Notes rise high, the heart takes flight,
In laughter's grasp, all feels so right.
Yet shadows linger, darkly cast,
A bittersweet refrain, unsurpassed.

Melodies weave through light and gloom,
A song of love, a hint of doom.
In every chord, a tale unfolds,
A tapestry of hearts so bold.

Twilight Brushstrokes of Emotion

The sky drips hues of deep remorse,
With colors bright, it finds its course.
Each brushstroke whispers of the night,
Where dreams take shape, both dark and light.

In twilight's hold, emotions spill,
Across the canvas, quiet, still.
A fleeting glance, a lingering sigh,
As shadows dance beneath the sky.

The Art of Wistful Farewells

Each parting brings a longing ache,
In whispered words, the heart will break.
Goodbyes are painted soft and slow,
An artist's touch where memories grow.

With every wave, a story told,
Of laughter shared and hands to hold.
In silence, echoes softly dwell,
The art resides in fond farewell.

Whispers of Joy in the Night

In shadows deep, where dreams take flight,
The stars above, a guiding light.
Soft echoes dance, in quiet tune,
Whispers of joy, beneath the moon.

Hearts entwined, in silence shared,
Moments linger, unprepared.
A gentle breeze, the night winds sigh,
In joy we find, the reasons why.

The Silent Symphony of Two Hearts

Two souls align, in perfect grace,
A silent tune, we both embrace.
Fingers touch like softest rain,
In this symphony, love's refrain.

Through every look, a note takes flight,
Harmony blooms in the soft night.
In every heartbeat, notes compose,
A melody only we know.

Crescendo of Hope and Heartbreak

A fragile note, the air holds tight,
Hope rises strong, but fades from sight.
In shadows cast by love's sweet game,
Heartbreak sings, yet never the same.

Through every tear, a story spun,
In twilight's glow, we come undone.
Yet from the ache, a spark ignites,
Crescendo builds on starry nights.

Tangles of Life's Sweetest Sorrow

Echoes of laughter, shadows of pain,
Life's winding path, a beautiful chain.
In tangled webs, our stories weave,
Sweetest sorrow, in hearts we believe.

Through storms we wander, we find our way,
In every night, there blooms a day.
Sorrow's kiss, a soft embrace,
Through every trial, we find our place.

Harmonies of Delight and Regret

In the garden where laughter blooms,
Forgotten whispers twist like fumes.
Sunlight dances on joyful days,
While shadows linger in faded ways.

Echoes of past joys softly chime,
Regrets entwined with the rings of time.
In moments bright, hearts intertwine,
Yet sorrow dwells on love's decline.

Songs of Light and Shadow

Beneath the glow of a golden sky,
Hopeful songs in the night drift by.
In every dawn, the light breaks free,
Yet shadows chase what we cannot see.

The moonlight whispers secrets true,
While darkness holds the pain we rue.
A symphony of night, a serenade,
In the balance, dreams are made.

Chants of Happiness and Grief

In laughter's song, our spirits rise,
Yet somewhere deep, a teardrop lies.
Joy sings sweetly in every heart,
While sorrow plays its quiet part.

We dance on paths of light and dark,
Each moment leaves its silent mark.
For every joy, there's loss to bear,
In this tapestry, we weave our care.

Verses of Cheer and Remorse

With every smile, the world spins bright,
Yet shadows linger, stealing light.
In laughter's echo, we find our way,
But whispers of sorrow come out to play.

The heart knows both bliss and regret,
In the tapestry of love, we fret.
We sing our joys but know too well,
The stories of sorrow that we can't tell.

Lyrical Moods of Elation and Pain

In joyous peaks, where laughter swells,
The heart sings bright, where magic dwells.
Yet shadows creep, with silent tread,
In whispers soft, they fill with dread.

For every smile that lights the day,
There lies a tear that fades away.
In fleeting joy, the thorns reside,
The dance of life, both pain and pride.

Ballad of the Broken and Beloved

Once held in arms, now lost in time,
A melody fades, a silent rhyme.
The heartbeats collide in memories,
In echoes soft, the love still frees.

A fragile tether, both strong and frail,
Two souls entangled, destined to sail.
Yet storms do rage, and winds do blow,
In wounds still fresh, sweet love does grow.

Bright Skies and Drifting Clouds

Underneath a vast blue dome,
The sun doth dance, the world's a home.
Yet clouds come drifting, shades of gray,
In fleeting moments, joy gives way.

With silver linings, hope we find,
Through trials faced, and fate entwined.
In every storm, a brighter dawn,
We learn to rise, with spirits drawn.

The Harmony of Hidden Tears

In silence kept, emotions flow,
A symphony of what we know.
A gentle ache, a quiet song,
In hidden depths, where hearts belong.

Each tear concealed, a note so true,
In harmony, the dark and blue.
Through strains of pain, the beauty gleams,
Life's fragile chords, are woven dreams.

Rhythms of Joyful Reminiscence

In golden fields, our laughter soared,
Fleeting moments, happily stored.
Each echo dances in my heart,
A symphony that won't depart.

Time weaves tales of days gone by,
Underneath the vast blue sky.
Memories twirl like autumn leaves,
Painting dreams that one believes.

The sunset blushes with our cheer,
In gentle whispers, I draw near.
A melody of times we spent,
In shadows cast, our love is lent.

Through twilight's hush, we find the grace,
In soft embraces, we interlace.
Rhythms play, in endless flow,
Together still, we deeply glow.

Diary of Blissful Shadows

In quiet corners of my mind,
I weave the threads of memories kind.
A diary kept in secret tones,
Where shadows dance and light condones.

Whispers linger in the night,
Soft confessions, pure delight.
Each page a phase, a moment's grace,
Evoking smiles on every face.

Golden hours in soft repose,
Smiles and giggles, fleeting prose.
With every line, a story spun,
Tales of laughter, heartbeats won.

In daylight's warmth, they flourish bright,
In twilight's arms, they take to flight.
A diary filled with dreams anew,
In shadows, blissful joys accrue.

Duets of Cheer and Pain

In harmony, the heartbeats blend,
A song of joy, a sorrow's end.
We dance where shadows mingle light,
In duets forged through day and night.

Every tear a note, a line,
Every laugh, a sunbeam's shine.
In balance, we find our refrain,
Embracing both the cheer and pain.

Through stormy skies, we rise and fall,
In the silence, we hear the call.
With every chord, a truth unfolds,
In stories whispered, love beholds.

Together, we write the symphony,
In every loss, we find the glee.
In duets of experiences true,
We learn from both the old and new.

Themes of Laughter and Mourning

In fleeting smiles and gentle sighs,
We weave the threads of our goodbyes.
A tapestry of joy and grief,
In memories, we seek relief.

The echo of laughter, sweet and clear,
Lingers softly, yet draws near.
In shadows of loss, the light still glows,
A tender reminder of what life shows.

Through tears we find the brightest spark,
In every journey, every dark.
Themes of laughter blend with pain,
In every season, love remains.

Though time may fade our fleeting years,
In every smile, we hold our tears.
In harmony, we face the dawn,
Themes of life—never truly gone.

Tones of Warmth and Chill

In the glow of sunset's light,
Warmth envelops the night.
Echoes of laughter fill the air,
Chill of dusk, a tender care.

Soft whispers dance in twilight's glow,
Sparks of joy, a gentle flow.
As shadows stretch and darkness looms,
The heart finds peace amidst the gloom.

Crimson skies begin to fade,
Colors blend, a sweet cascade.
Winter's breath, a fleeting sigh,
Promises whispered as time flies by.

Whispered Ballads of Joy and Farewell

In the soft glow of morning light,
Joy unfolds, a pure delight.
Songs of laughter fill the air,
Whispered loves, beyond compare.

Tender memories gently weave,
In every word, we believe.
As shadows gather, hearts entwined,
Farewell's note, bittersweet and kind.

A melody of dreams takes flight,
In the stillness of the night.
Though goodbyes bring a tearful grace,
In every ending, a warm embrace.

Melodies of Joy and Heartache

In the morning's gentle glow,
Joyful whispers start to flow.
Harmonies in the softest breeze,
Chasing worries, setting peace.

Yet as the sun descends so low,
Heartache drifts, a fleeting woe.
Melodies linger, bittersweet,
In every sorrow, love's heartbeat.

Stars above begin to shine,
In darkness, hope is intertwined.
Through joy and pain, we find our way,
In melodies that softly play.

Sonnet of Smiles Beneath Clouded Skies

Beneath the clouds, a smile takes flight,
A spark of joy, though shadows loom bright.
In every tear, a story does unfold,
A tapestry of warmth, woven in gold.

Through the haze, glimmers of hope appear,
Whispers of laughter, banishing fear.
In the heart's garden, flowers still bloom,
Even in silence, love conquers the gloom.

Cadence of Warmth and Cold

Winds of winter, chill to the bone,
Yet hearts ignite with a warmth of their own.
Between the seasons, a dance unfolds,
Embracing the heat, as the frost scolds.

In quiet moments, two spirits collide,
Finding connection where warmth does abide.
Through the tempest, they weather each storm,
In every heartbeat, a silence transforms.

Stanzas of Elation and Desolation

In the heights, pure joy does reside,
While in valleys, sorrow may hide.
Yet through the struggles, life finds its song,
In echoes of laughter, we all belong.

From peaks of elation to depths full of pain,
The journey continues through sunshine and rain.
For every shadow, there's light to embrace,
In the duality, we all find our place.

Musings of Laughter Amidst Grief

In the heart of darkness, laughter will glow,
A beacon of hope, in the depths of sorrow.
Through memories cherished, we find a way,
To honor the past in the light of today.

Each chuckle a whisper of love still near,
In moments of silence, we carry the cheer.
Though grief may linger, joy takes its ground,
In the dance of remembrance, solace is found.

Whispers Beneath the Stars

Underneath the endless night,
Soft secrets dance in gentle flight.
Stars above us gleam and twinkle,
In the silence, hearts do crinkle.

Each whisper carries dreams untold,
Stories woven, truths of old.
As the breeze wraps 'round our forms,
The universe in beauty warms.

In shadows cast by moonlit beams,
We find solace in our dreams.
Connected by the twinkling light,
Together, we embrace the night.

Echoes of Laughter and Tears

In laughter's echo, joy takes flight,
Moments captured, hearts feel light.
Yet shadows linger, soft and near,
For every smile, a hint of tears.

Memories weave a tender thread,
In stories shared, where hearts are led.
Between the laughter, silence sighs,
And every tear reflects the skies.

Through the highs and lows we roam,
Our hearts find solace in the foam.
In every moment, lessons gleam,
A tapestry sewn from hope and dream.

The Dance of Light and Shadow

In twilight's grace, the shadows play,
As daylight slowly slips away.
A dance begins where contrasts meet,
In every pulse, a heartbeat sweet.

Light paints the world in golden hues,
While shadows whisper hidden clues.
Together they weave stories bold,
In every flicker, life unfolds.

We drift between the dark and bright,
Finding beauty in day and night.
In this ballet of time and fate,
We learn to love, to live, relate.

Ballads of Heartfelt Longing

In the stillness, hearts confide,
Yearning whispers carried wide.
A melody of love's sweet song,
In every note, we feel we belong.

Across the distance, dreams ignite,
Lighting paths in the darkest night.
With every heartbeat, a promise gleams,
Life's canvas painted with hopes and dreams.

Yet time can stretch, and space can bend,
In each heartbeat, we transcend.
These ballads echo, deep and true,
In every longing, I reach for you.

The Quietude After a Storm

The clouds drift slowly away,
Leaves whisper tales of old.
Raindrops twinkle in the sun,
Nature's breath, soft and bold.

The air is fresh, a gentle sigh,
Birds return, their songs arise.
Each corner glimmers with life,
Underneath the vast blue skies.

Puddles mirror waking trees,
Sunlight dances on the ground.
In the calm, new dreams are born,
Beauty in stillness is found.

A world renewed, the heart beats slow,
In this moment, peace will grow.
From chaos springs a silent grace,
Time stands still in this embrace.

Mournful Ballads of Love

In the shadows, memories weep,
Soft words spoken, now echoes stray.
Each glance holds a story deep,
Love once bright, now fades away.

Whispers linger in the night,
Promises lost in bitter air.
Dreams we shared, a fleeting light,
Now just ghosts that haunt the fare.

Silver tears on lonely cheeks,
Every heartbeat, a silent plea.
Hopes once high, now feeling weak,
Shadows dance where we used to be.

Yet in sorrow, beauty lies,
In the ache, a tender trace.
Love's lament, beneath the skies,
Mournful ballads, time can't erase.

Radiant Echoes of the Heart

When laughter rings like silver chimes,
And joy spills out in vibrant hues,
Each heartbeat sings of endless times,
A melody that feels like news.

With every glance, a spark ignites,
Eyes meet, and worlds start to spin.
Radiant dreams take dazzling flights,
Whispers warm, like the summer's skin.

In gentle moments, magic sways,
Every word, a tender art.
Through tangled paths and winding ways,
Together we create the heart.

Echoes linger, bright and clear,
In the dance of love's sweet song.
With open arms, we draw near,
In radiant fields, we belong.

The Tug of Happiness and Heartache

In laughter's arms, we bask in light,
Yet shadows follow close behind.
The tug of joy, a fleeting flight,
With heartache's weight intertwined.

Moments sparkle, but time will bend,
Each smile hides a whispered pain.
In the chaos, broken mends,
Life's sweet sunshine, streaked with rain.

A bittersweet song plays on repeat,
Each note bittersweet, yet so dear.
The dance of love, both fast and fleet,
A tender pull of hope and fear.

Through the highs and all the lows,
We weave our tales, a fragile thread.
In this dance, we learn and grow,
A tapestry of love, of dread.

Whispers of Joy and Longing

In the stillness of night, hearts sway,
Soft whispers dance in the moon's soft ray.
Dreams flutter gently, hopes take flight,
Yearning for moments, tender and bright.

The laughter of children fills the air,
While shadows linger, a silent prayer.
Life's sweet chorus, a bittersweet song,
In echoes of joy, where we belong.

Time weaves stories, both near and far,
Guiding our hearts like a distant star.
Underneath the stars, desires ignite,
Whispers of joy chase the shades of night.

Yet longing remains, a shadowy trace,
A dance of emotions, a tender embrace.
In the fragments of dreams, we find our way,
Whispers of love brighten the day.

Ballads of Laughter and Tears

In the heart of laughter, a tale unfolds,
With echoes of warmth, and secrets untold.
Joy weaves its magic, like threads in a loom,
While shadows of sorrow can darken the room.

Children's giggles rise high in the breeze,
While sorrows whisper, begging for ease.
In moments of laughter, joy takes the lead,
Yet tears drop softly, like rain on a seed.

Together they dance, both heavy and light,
A melody formed between day and night.
For every bright smile, a sorrow may hide,
In ballads of life, both joy and tears glide.

Through valleys of laughter, through mountains of grief,
We find ourselves planted, in beliefs so brief.
In the tapestry woven by heartstrings entwined,
Ballads of laughter and tears are defined.

Echoes of Grins and Heartaches

Amid the shadows, a grin takes flight,
Chasing the heartache that lingers at night.
In moments so fleeting, we find our truth,
Echoes of laughter, fragments of youth.

Every smile carries a whisper of pain,
Woven together like sunshine and rain.
In the tangled tapestry of life's embrace,
Heartaches remind us of love's gentle grace.

With every heartbeat, a story unfurls,
Echoing softly as life twirls and whirls.
Each grin a reminder of battles once fought,
Heartaches a lesson that time surely taught.

We rise with the dawn, to face what may come,
With echoes of grins, we won't come undone.
For in every heartache, a lesson is sown,
Echoes of grins will lead us back home.

Melodies of Bliss and Despair

In the hush of the night, melodies play,
Tales of bliss weaving through shadows of gray.
Each note a heartbeat, a sigh in the breeze,
Whispers of joy mixed with longing that frees.

Dancing through valleys, where dreams intertwine,
Despair lingers lightly, like a soft, cautioned sign.
Yet in the silence, beauty finds its way,
Melodies born from both night and the day.

In the rhythm of life, we sway to the tune,
Balancing moments like sun and the moon.
Through joy and through pain, we find our refrain,
Melodies humming through pleasure and pain.

Together we sing, a harmony pure,
In the depths of despair, love will endure.
For every heartbeat, a melody shared,
In bliss and in sorrow, we find we are paired.

Notes from the Heart's Crypt

In shadows deep, where memories lie,
Old whispers echo, a soft goodbye.
Each letter penned with yearning strife,
A relic of love, a fragment of life.

Dusty wishes, wrapped in despair,
Held close to the heart, laid painfully bare.
Ghosts of laughter drift in the air,
In the crypt of emotions, we find what's rare.

Ink-stained secrets, hidden from light,
Breathe life to dreams that fade from sight.
In the stillness, sweet shadows play,
Tracing the paths where our hearts went astray.

With every sorrow, a lesson learned,
In the heart's crypt, the flame still burned.
We gather the pieces, both near and far,
In the echoes of love, we find who we are.

Glittering Isles of Joy and Woe

Across the sea where the sun meets the tide,
Glittering isles, where secrets reside.
Joy dances lightly on the crests of the waves,
While shadows deepen in the hidden caves.

Laughter flutters on the ocean's breeze,
But sorrow lingers beneath the trees.
Each isle a story, a dance of fate,
With hearts entwined, both fragile and great.

Stars are scattered like dreams on the shore,
While tides of change push us evermore.
In the pulse of the water, our spirits collide,
On glittering isles where love and pain bide.

Through joy we blossom, through woe we learn,
In life's rich tapestry, we twist and turn.
A journey of hearts, of laughter and sighs,
In the glittering isles where our truth never lies.

Torn Pages of a Luminous Past

In the book of time, pages fray,
Torn by the hands that strove to stay.
Each chapter whispered, a tale of light,
In the luminous past, we claim our right.

Memories flicker like candles aglow,
Some bring warmth, while others bestow.
Lessons scattered like petals in spring,
From the torn pages, our souls take wing.

Echoes of laughter, soft as a sigh,
While shadows beckon, we still reach high.
In the heart's library, time's endless cast,
We write our futures from the stories amassed.

Though pages may tear, and ink may fade,
In the tapestry woven, love is displayed.
We gather the fragments, the bright and the grim,
From the torn pages, our lives fill to the brim.

The Subtle Art of Heartstrings

With gentle fingers, we pluck the strings,
Creating melodies of the heart that sings.
Each note a whisper, tender and true,
In the subtle art of the love we pursue.

Rhythms entwine in a delicate dance,
Painting the silence, igniting romance.
In harmony's grasp, we find our release,
The subtle art that brings us peace.

Moments like raindrops on a window pane,
Echoes of joy mixed with hints of pain.
In the symphony played by souls intertwined,
The heartstrings awaken, the past redefined.

Through trials and triumphs, we compose our song,
In the quietest places, where we belong.
In the subtle art, our spirits align,
Our heartstrings resound, forever divine.

The Poignancy of Silent Laughter

In a room where shadows blend,
Soft whispers drift without an end.
Eyes gleam with untold tales,
A quiet joy that never fails.

Each smile hides a weighty sigh,
A secret world where dreams can fly.
Together in a still embrace,
Silent laughter fills the space.

Unspoken bonds, both strong and light,
Illuminate the deepest night.
A gentle echo, warm and bright,
In silence, hearts take flight.

So let us cherish what is shared,
In moments when the world is spared.
For in the hush, love's truth can gleam,
A poignant place, a whispered dream.

Amidst the Echoing Shadows

Beneath the trees where whispers play,
Shadows dance through light of day.
Every rustle tells a tale,
Of hopes and dreams that softly sail.

Echoes linger in the air,
Memories held with tender care.
In every sigh, a history,
In every glance, a mystery.

Lost in thoughts that intertwine,
Where dusk and dawn begin to shine.
The past and present, hand in hand,
Together craft a timeless land.

Amidst the echoes, life will bloom,
In shaded corners, dispelling gloom.
With every heartbeat, shadows sway,
In this dance of night and day.

An Elegy for Moments Lost

Upon the pages time unfolds,
Our fleeting moments, stories told.
Each laugh a bell that fades away,
A whisper in the light of day.

What once was bright now dims to gray,
In memories where shadows play.
A gentle ache, a fragile thread,
For everything that has been said.

We mourn the laughter, the sweet embrace,
A waltz of dreams we cannot trace.
Yet in the heart, those echoes lie,
A timeless song that cannot die.

So let us hold the fleeting bliss,
The moments wrapped in tender kiss.
Though lost in time, we keep them close,
An elegy to what we chose.

The Canvas of Love's Paradoxes

Painted skies in hues of fate,
Where love and sorrow tightly wait.
Bright strokes clash with muted tears,
Creating art from hopes and fears.

Every touch, a brush of pain,
In vibrant colors, joy and stain.
A puzzle where each piece aligns,
In shadows deep, the light still shines.

We weave a fabric, rich and rare,
With threads of bliss and threads of care.
In silence held, the loudest cries,
A paradox beneath the skies.

So let us roam this canvas wide,
With every heartbeat as our guide.
For in love's dance, both dark and bright,
We find the art in day and night.

Rhapsody in Light and Dark

In shadows dance the glowing sparks,
Whispers faint as night embarks.
Light entwines with dark's embrace,
Creating music, time and space.

Echoes of the moon's soft grace,
Stars ignite in a cosmic chase.
A tapestry of twilight's hue,
Where dreams are born and fears subdue.

Sunrise paints the canvas wide,
Chasing off the fear inside.
Yet dusk brings a soothing balm,
In its chill, a quiet calm.

To walk between both realms we find,
A harmony to soothe the mind.
In rhapsody, we weave our fate,
In light and dark, we celebrate.

Lullabies of Exultation and Sorrow

Softly sing the night's sweet tune,
Beneath the watchful, silver moon.
Joy cascades like falling stars,
Yet sorrow's shadow leaves its scars.

Whispers linger in the skies,
In every laugh, a hidden sigh.
Singing lullabies, we blend,
The joy and grief that life can send.

In gentle waves, the heart does sway,
Through laughter's light and sorrow's way.
Each note a tear, a smile's grace,
We find our peace in time and space.

Wrapped in warmth, we drift away,
To dream of night, and hope for day.
In lullabies of joy and woe,
We learn to let our soft hearts glow.

Odes of Laughter's Embrace

Upon the breeze, a giggle flies,
A chorus born of bright blue skies.
Each chuckle dances, light and free,
A melody for hearts at ease.

Joyful echoes fill the air,
With every grin, we cast our care.
In laughter's arms, we find our way,
Chasing shadows, come what may.

Together in this radiant bliss,
A moment shared, we dare not miss.
Holding tight to joy's sweet taste,
In laughter's embrace, there's no waste.

As life unfolds, we sing our song,
In laughter's warmth, we all belong.
These odes of cheer, we gladly share,
In life's great play, we show we care.

Ballads of Hope and Melancholy

In twilight's glow, we weave our tales,
Of dreams that rise, and weary sails.
A melody of hopes that soar,
Yet echoes of what was before.

In every stroke of fate's own hand,
We sing of hills where rivers stand.
A balance found in gentle strife,
In sorrow's teach, we uncover life.

The heart can hold both joy and pain,
In every flower, a hint of rain.
Yet through the clouds, the sun will break,
In ballads sung, our souls awake.

With every note, we hold the night,
Illuminated by stars so bright.
In hope and melancholy's dance,
We find our truth, we take our chance.

Sonnet of Joyful Farewells

In laughter shared, we part this day,
With smiles that dance, and hearts at play.
A chapter ends, yet memories stay,
In the warmth of bonds, we find our way.

Though paths may twist and times may change,
Our souls entwined will not derange.
In every hug, the love's exchange,
This joy we feel is not so strange.

With bright horizons near and wide,
Embrace the future, let dreams guide.
In every tear, let hope reside,
For every end, there's joy inside.

So raise a glass to all we've known,
In this sweet moment, we have grown.
Let laughter echo, love be shown,
A joyful farewell, we've brightly sown.

When Sunlight Meets Rain

When sunlight greets the teardrops' fall,
A bridge appears, a vibrant wall.
The sky ignites in colors bright,
As joy and sorrow dance in light.

Each droplet brings the earth a chance,
In nature's arms, a blissful trance.
The flowers bloom, the world revives,
In harmony, the spirit thrives.

The raindrops whisper on the leaves,
While sunlight weaves through golden eaves.
They share a story, soft and sweet,
In every moment, life's heartbeat.

Together, they create a hue,
Of hope and love, forever true.
When shadows fade, and skies are clear,
Sunlight and rain will always cheer.

A Symphony of Dreams and Dilemmas

In twilight's gaze, dreams softly call,
Yet shadows linger, doubts enthrall.
A melody of wishes hums,
While echoes of the past still strum.

In every choice, a chance to rise,
The heart, a compass that defies.
With every step, a rhythm starts,
A symphony that stirs our hearts.

Listen closely, the tunes may blend,
Where dreams begin, and fears suspend.
With hope as notes and pain as rest,
We find our way through every quest.

In life's grand stage, both light and shade,
Create a song, a grand parade.
In melodies, we find our fate—
A dance of dreams, we celebrate.

Verses Woven in Grief

In quiet moments, shadows weep,
The echoes of your voice we keep.
Each memory, like threads do bind,
A tapestry of love combined.

In whispered winds, your laughter sings,
Through stormy nights, the comfort brings.
Yet sorrow lingers, deep and wide,
In every tear we've had to hide.

The heart holds weight of what we've lost,
Yet love persists, no matter cost.
With every heartbeat, you are near,
In woven verses, I hold dear.

So let the world remember still,
The essence of your strength and will.
In every breath, your spirit thrives,
Through woven grief, the love survives.

The Heart's Dual Facade

In silence, walls begin to rise,
A tender mask that often lies.
Joy's laughter dances, bright and bold,
While sorrow whispers, quiet and cold.

Two faces twirl upon the stage,
Each one a tale, a different page.
One seeks light, the other shade,
In each embrace, life's truths are laid.

A heart is pulled, a constant fight,
To find the warmth in darkest night.
A flicker dims, then shines anew,
In every heartbeat, shades of blue.

Yet through the storm, hope holds its ground,
In every peak, the valleys found.
With wings unfurled, the heart will soar,
Embracing both, forevermore.

Luminous Flickers of Sadness

Soft glimmers dance in twilight's grace,
A cherished tear upon the face.
Stars above, in whispered glow,
Reflect the depths of pain we know.

Each flicker tells a tale of light,
Beneath the dark, the heart ignites.
In shadows deep, a spark remains,
A thread of hope amidst the pains.

Memories linger, bittersweet,
In every pulse, they find their beat.
While joy invites, the sorrow stays,
In fragile moments, life displays.

Yet through the haze, a beauty gleams,
In every crack, a light redeems.
With open arms, we hold the night,
For in the dark, we find our light.

Chasing Shadows of Laughter

Hidden echoes roam the hall,
Chasing laughter's fleeting call.
Once a shout, now a sigh,
In sweet pursuit, we wonder why.

Where joy once bloomed, now shadows creep,
In memory's arms, we safely keep.
A fleeting smile, a ghostly trace,
We search for warmth in an empty space.

Through winding paths of lost delight,
We weave the threads that keep us tight.
A dance of shadows, light retreats,
Yet laughter lingers, soft heartbeats.

Embrace the echoes, let them glide,
For in the chase, true hearts abide.
With every step, we learn to find,
Joy intertwined, forever blind.

Capturing Moments of Ephemeral Joy

A fleeting glance, a smile betwixt,
In moments brief, life's magic fixed.
Petals fall, like whispers soft,
In rented time, we dance aloft.

Each second glows with golden rays,
In simple acts, the heart obeys.
Hands entwined beneath the sun,
In transient bliss, two souls are one.

Captured moments, like fireflies,
Illuminate the evening skies.
In laughter shared, our spirits play,
A glimpse of joy that won't decay.

Though time may steal, and shadows blend,
These memories linger, never end.
For every heartbeat writes a story,
In ephemeral joy, we find our glory.

Lyrics of Radiance and Woe

In the dawn, the sun does rise,
Casting light on hopeful skies.
Yet shadows creep, a tale untold,
Whispers of hearts, both brave and bold.

In laughter's glow, we dance and sing,
The joy of life, a radiant fling.
But tears may fall, like silver rain,
Echoes of love, entwined with pain.

Each heartbeat counts, a fleeting song,
It carries us, both right and wrong.
As day turns dusk, the light will fade,
Leaving behind the dreams we've made.

With every spark, there comes a tear,
In this world, so bright yet drear.
We'll grasp the joy, endure the fear,
In lyrics of woe that draw us near.

Serenades of Delight and Loss

With melodies that float on air,
Delightful notes beyond compare.
Yet in the chorus lies a sigh,
A tender loss, a fleeting fly.

In twilight's embrace, laughter rings,
Celebrating all the joy it brings.
Yet in the silence, echoes bloom,
Memories weave a subtle gloom.

The stars above, a sparkling train,
Each twinkle holds a thread of pain.
For every joy, a shadow cast,
In serenades, the die is cast.

Together found, then lost anew,
In every song, a hint of blue.
Delight and loss dance hand in hand,
A bittersweet but wondrous band.

Anthems of Ecstasy and Gloom

Raise your voice to the heavens bright,
An anthem sung in pure delight.
In moments grand, we lose control,
Boundless joy that fills the soul.

Yet shadows linger, dark and deep,
A haunting echo, secrets keep.
In every rise, a chance to fall,
The dance of life, a muted call.

From joyous peaks to valleys low,
We seek the light, the undertow.
In every heartbeat, a pulse of time,
With ecstasy and gloom, we climb.

Embrace the thrill, the fleeting taste,
Of life's sweet nectar, never waste.
For every joy that makes us bloom,
We carry forth our deepest gloom.

Chronicles of Grins and Cries

In every smile, a story lies,
A mix of laughter, love, and sighs.
For life's a canvas, shades entwined,
In chronicles where hearts are blind.

Beneath the grins, the shadows play,
In silent cries that fade away.
With every jest, a tear concealed,
In joyful moments, pain revealed.

From fleeting joy to lasting strife,
We scribble tales of this sweet life.
With grins that shine and cries that flow,
We dance through time, our hearts aglow.

In each embrace, a tear may gleam,
A reflection of a cherished dream.
In chronicles, we laugh and weep,
The stories blend, both vast and deep.

Contrasts of Sorrowful Sunshine

Golden rays peek through the gloom,
Casting light on shadows' tomb.
Whispers of warmth disdain the cold,
Yet stories of grief silently unfold.

The flowers bloom with vibrant hue,
While hearts bear burdens, old and new.
In laughter's wake, sadness lingers,
Joy slips through grasp like scattered fingers.

Bright skies veil the tears that fall,
In sunlight's glare, we feel it all.
The contrast sharp, yet tender still,
In sorrow's grip, the light can thrill.

Beneath the sun, the shadows dance,
Life's fleeting moments blend by chance.
With every sigh, a story penned,
In contrast lies the heart's true mend.

The Gentle Pull of Grief's Embrace

In quiet corners, sorrows dwell,
A heavy heart, a whispered yell.
Time drips slowly, heavy like rain,
Each drop a memory, deepening pain.

Wrapped in shadows, soft and tight,
Grief's embrace pulls through the night.
Yet in this sorrow, love survives,
A bitter-sweetness that truly thrives.

Faces linger in the misty air,
Echoes of laughter echo despair.
With every pulse, a tender ache,
In grief's soft hold, we gently break.

But from this grief, we rise again,
A testament of love through pain.
For in each tear, a strength we find,
The gentle pull of hearts entwined.

Rhapsody of Unspoken Dreams

Beneath the stars, our dreams take flight,
In silence loud, they seek the light.
Whispers linger, hopes unshared,
In the quiet, we are bared.

Each heartbeat dances in the dark,
Yearnings sparkle, a hidden spark.
The melodies of wishes soar,
Yet fear holds tight, and dreams ignore.

In the shadows, secrets sigh,
The rhapsody of what and why.
With every thought, a world unfolds,
In silence wrapped, the heart beholds.

To speak of dreams, a fearless quest,
Yet deep inside, we hide the best.
In rhapsody, our souls collide,
No longer lost, we turn the tide.

The Sighs Between the Notes

In melodies where silence breathes,
The sighs between the notes we seize.
A song is more than sound alone,
It's every whisper, every groan.

The pauses hold a tale untold,
In stillness, warmth can turn to cold.
With every rest, a longing wakes,
A harmony that bends and breaks.

The rhythm flows, but shadows creep,
In every note, a secret we keep.
For music's heart is not just bright,
It holds the echoes of the night.

So listen deep, for all that's felt,
In sighs between, our truths are dealt.
In every chord, a story stays,
The sighs between weave life's necessary ways.

Whirlwind of Tenderness and Loss

In a storm of sighs and soft goodbyes,
Memories whisper, the heart softly cries.
Each moment cherished, yet fleeting in flight,
Tenderness lingers, lost in the night.

Clouds rush with shadows, pain weathered deep,
Embers of love in the silence we keep.
The whirlwind spins, a dance of regret,
In every turn, a tale we forget.

Hands once entwined now drift far apart,
The echoes of laughter still stir in the heart.
Yet in the chaos, the warmth still exists,
A touch of remembrance in every missed kiss.

Through the tempest's roar and the gentle hush,
We carry both sorrow and joy in the rush.
In this whirlwind, we find what we seek,
Tenderness blossoms amid all the bleak.

Tracing the Lines of Joy and Pain

With every heartbeat, a secret lays bare,
Tracing the lines of our laughter and care.
Joy dances lightly on the edge of despair,
In the tapestry woven with threads of our prayer.

Faded photographs caught in the light,
Moments preserved, both fragile and bright.
In the ink of our tears, the colors combine,
Creating a portrait of both joy and sign.

Each scar a reminder, each smile a song,
Navigating feelings, where both belong.
In the garden of hearts, where thorns intertwine,
We learn to embrace both the bitter and fine.

With fingers that trace every curve of our past,
We find in the struggle, a love that will last.
Joy and pain dance in exquisite embrace,
Together they paint our eternal grace.

Notes of the In-Between

In the hush of the twilight, whispers align,
Notes of the in-between carry secrets divine.
Between dreams and waking, life's rhythms unfold,
The stories of warmth in the rapture of cold.

Crisp echoes linger like ghosts in the air,
Each note a reminder, a moment to share.
Between hopes and fears, a melody plays,
Carving the silence in delicate ways.

Fleeting glances caught in a meaningful glance,
In the space left behind lies an unspoken chance.
Notes of the in-between serenade the soul,
Binding the fragments that make us whole.

In the quiet, we find a symphony sweet,
The harmony found in each heart's gentle beat.
With every heartbeat, we write our own score,
In the in-between, we dance evermore.

The Quiet Lullaby of Remnants

In twilight's embrace, the remnants do sing,
A quiet lullaby on the breath of spring.
Whispers of what was, gently entwined,
In memories linger, the essence defined.

Soft shadows glide through the evening's soft glow,
Carrying stories that ebb and that flow.
In each fading echo, a promise we trace,
The quiet of loss reveals hidden grace.

Through the stillness, a heartbeat remains,
Lullabies murmuring through joys and through pains.
In the hush of the night, the past intertwines,
The remnants of love in invisible lines.

As stars flicker softly, casting their lights,
The lullaby beckons on clear, fragrant nights.
In the quiet, we find comfort in all,
The remnants of life in the night's gentle call.

Cadence of Joy and Sorrow

In the morning light, laughter soars,
Yet shadows linger, knocking on doors.
The dance of smiles, a fleeting glimpse,
While tears carve paths, like quiet imprints.

Joy blossoms bright in the springtime air,
But winter comes, leaving no one to spare.
Each heartbeat sings a bittersweet tune,
A melody woven with sun and the moon.

The sun sets low, painting skies gray,
And whispers of hope drift slowly away.
Yet in the night, stars find their chance,
To twinkle and shimmer, a cosmic dance.

Cradled in shadows, we learn to embrace,
Both joy and sorrow in life's tender face.
For in the fusion of laughter and pain,
We find our strength, our truth's last refrain.

Fleeting Echoes of Yesterday

Memories linger, like whispers in time,
Each echo breathes life to a forgotten rhyme.
We chase the shadows, we yearn to revive,
The flickering moments that once made us thrive.

Red leaves are falling, the seasons they change,
Yet faces we loved feel somehow estranged.
A photograph glimmers, a smile within,
But time moves on, unfurling its skin.

Soft rains remind us of laughter so sweet,
As footsteps resound on a familiar street.
With every glance back, we gather the shards,
Of joy and of heartache, our own little guards.

The past is a tapestry, woven with care,
Each thread a reminder, a moment we share.
And though it may fade like the dusk in the sky,
Its essence remains as we learn to fly.

Dichotomy of Smiles and Frowns

A grin may mask a hidden concern,
Yet joy can ignite the heart's slow burn.
In the dance of life, we play our part,
Crafting our faces, concealing the heart.

In laughter's embrace, sorrow may hide,
A testament of the heart's gentle tide.
We wander through gardens of beauty and strife,
Navigating the edges that carve out our life.

With each fleeting smile, a story unfolds,
A tale of the present, of futures untold.
Yet frowns carry weight, like shadows of night,
A balance we bear between softness and light.

In the duality, we find our refrain,
Both joy and despair, like sun and like rain.
For smiles and frowns are but two sides of one,
A mirror reflecting the journey begun.

Serenades of Hope and Despondence

Between the heartbeats, where silence resides,
Hope flickers gently, in whispers it hides.
Yet shadows loom heavy, a cloak made of fears,
Each note of despair drips like rain from the years.

Songs of the night cradle dreams that we chase,
While thoughts of the past linger, a soft embrace.
Each chord resonates, an echo so true,
A serenade woven from sorrow and blue.

Yet dawn breaks slowly, igniting the skies,
With hues of resilience where promise surely lies.
In the symphony crafted with love and with pain,
We learn to dance softly in sunshine and rain.

For hope is a melody, sweet in its sound,
In the midst of despondence, new dreams can be found.
With each fleeting moment, our spirits will rise,
In the concert of life, where each blessing complies.

Reflections in Glee and Sorrow

In the mirror of light, joy dances bright,
Yet shadows creep softly, sealing the night.
Echoes of laughter, then whispers of pain,
A tapestry woven with sunshine and rain.

Moments of bliss like a fleeting dream,
Yet tears turn to pearls in the silver stream.
We stand at the crossroads of joy and despair,
Reflecting on what we have lost, what we share.

Each heartbeat a rhythm, a story to tell,
Of love that has thrived and of hearts that fell.
In glee, we find solace, in sorrow, we gain,
The colors of life painting pleasure and pain.

Through dusk and through dawn, we chase the divine,
With each glance behind, our souls intertwine.
In the tapestry of moments, both light and the dark,
We find in reflections, a resonant spark.

Rhymes of Radiant Smiles

In the morning's embrace, where laughter begins,
Radiant smiles shimmer, where true joy spins.
With each word we share, the world feels alive,
In the dance of connection, our spirits will thrive.

Moments like bubbles, so fragile, yet bright,
Carry whispers of happiness, pure delight.
In the warmth of our hearts, love's gentle refrain,
We find in the laughter, the cure for the pain.

Under the sun, every shadow retreats,
In the light of our joy, the darkness depletes.
Together we echo, in sweet harmony,
A symphony of smiles, forever carefree.

With each step we take, let's cherish the grace,
Of laughter and love, in this beautiful space.
For rhymes of our joy, let our voices soar high,
In the embrace of happiness, the soul learns to fly.

Cantos of Uplift and Heartbreak

In the twilight of dreams, our stories unfold,
Cantos of uplift, both tender and bold.
With each string we strum, a note lingers long,
A dance through the heart, in the rhythm of song.

From heights of elation to valleys of grief,
We traverse the landscape, seeking relief.
In echoes of heartache, we find our true song,
The melody of resilience, where we all belong.

In shadows, we gather the lessons we learn,
With every heartbreak, the fires burn.
Yet amidst the sorrow, a light always glows,
Cantos of passion that only time knows.

For every tear shed, a star's light will rise,
As we sing our own story beneath endless skies.
In the beauty of contrast, we find our way clear,
Cantos of uplift, through every hidden tear.

Notes of Joy and Droplets of Sadness

In the symphony of life, joy plays its tune,
With notes that resonate, like a sweet summer's noon.
Yet droplets of sadness fall soft as the rain,
In the heart's gentle rhythm, both pleasure and pain.

Every burst of laughter, a spark in the night,
Yet shadows surround, dimming flickering light.
In the dance of our hearts, emotions entwine,
An orchestra playing, both divine and benign.

From whispers of heartache to echoes of cheer,
Each note tells a story; each moment is dear.
As we weave through our days, in joy, we find grace,
While droplets of sadness leave a bittersweet trace.

Embrace the duality, let the music resound,
For in every heartbeat, life's treasures are found.
With notes of elation and tears that enhance,
We create our own melody, joining the dance.

When Laughter Fades to Silence

When laughter fades into the night,
Shadows deepen, dimming light.
Ghosts of joy begin to linger,
Silence wraps like a cold finger.

Memories drift on a distant breeze,
Echoes whispered through bare trees.
An empty room, the clock ticks slow,
The heart reflects on all we know.

Yet within the stillness, hope does bloom,
In hushed corners of the room.
For every silence has its song,
A promise that we still belong.

So when the laughter fades away,
Remember nights that turned to day.
In quiet times, the soul can sway,
And find new laughter on the way.

Notes from the Soul's Abyss

In deep shadows where feelings hide,
The heart's whispers often bide.
Fingers trace the lines of pain,
Each note speaks in a silent refrain.

Words unspoken weigh like stones,
In the depths, they're not alone.
Ink spills from a tortured heart,
A melody, both fierce and tart.

Yet there, amid the dark despair,
A flicker glimmers, soft as air.
It calls to rise, to meet the light,
To weave the shadows into bright.

From the abyss, a tune will soar,
A symphony of rich folklore.
Each note a step, a pathway clear,
From silence into something dear.

The Weaving of Delighted Dreams

In twilight's glow, the stars align,
Weaving dreams, a thread divine.
With every sigh, a tale begins,
As hope and wonder blend within.

Delighted thoughts take joyful flight,
On gossamer wings through the night.
Whispers dance with fragrant blooms,
In the garden where magic looms.

A tapestry of colors bright,
Stitched with laughter, pure delight.
Each moment captured, sewn with care,
In every heart, a dream to share.

So take my hand, let's chase the beams,
And nurture all our wildest dreams.
Together we shall spin the thread,
In this world where joy is spread.

The Soundtrack of Love's Journey

In the silence, soft notes arise,
Love's melody fills the skies.
Every heartbeat, a rhythmic song,
Guiding souls as they belong.

With each gaze, a furtive glance,
Two souls sway in a tender dance.
Fingers brush, a spark ignites,
The soundtrack plays through starry nights.

Through storm and calm, the music swells,
In whispered tones, our story dwells.
A harmony that knows no end,
In every note, we learn to bend.

So let the world compose anew,
The soundtrack of me and you.
In every moment, let love sing,
A symphony of everything.

Tides of Bliss and Despair

The ocean whispers secrets low,
As waves of joy begin to flow.
Yet shadows linger, dark and deep,
In tides of sorrow, hearts do weep.

A dance of light, a play of dark,
Each crest and trough, a fragile arc.
We ride the currents, fast and slow,
In bliss we find where sorrows go.

The moonlit tides, they shimmer bright,
Yet storms may brew, obscuring light.
A blend of laughter, pain, and bliss,
In every rise, a hopeful kiss.

So sail the seas of joy and dread,
In every ebb, the tears we've shed.
For in the depths, we learn to cope,
Amidst the tides, we find our hope.

Chords of Solace and Grief

A melody of sweet refrain,
Sings soft of love, yet hints of pain.
In every note, a story swells,
Of joys embraced and sorrowed bells.

The heartstrings tug, they pull and sway,
In chords that echo night and day.
With harmonies of loss and gain,
We find the solace wrapped in grain.

Each strum reveals the veil of time,
A tapestry of rhythm, rhyme.
In shadows cast, we find our light,
In grief's embrace, we dare to fight.

So play the strings, let music flow,
In every heart, the seeds we sow.
With chords of life, we rise and fall,
In solace sought, we stand up tall.

Reflections in the Moonlight

Beneath the gaze of silver beams,
The world transforms in quiet dreams.
Each ripple whispers tales untold,
Of hidden hopes, both brave and bold.

The stillness breathes, a gentle sigh,
As stars align in velvet sky.
In moonlit pools, our shadows dance,
With every glance, a fleeting chance.

The night's embrace, a tender touch,
In whispered secrets that mean so much.
So let your thoughts drift in the night,
And find your peace in soft moonlight.

A moment's pause, a heart laid bare,
In silence speaks the love we share.
Reflections of what lies within,
In moonbeam's glow, our journeys begin.

Harmonies of Hope and Regret

In every heartbeat, a song we weave,
Of love once lost, and dreams we believe.
Through echoes of laughter, whispers of pain,
In harmonies sweet, we rise once again.

The past may haunt, but still we sing,
Of futures bright, and the hope they bring.
As notes intertwine, they create a space,
Where sorrow meets joy in a warm embrace.

Each chord a lesson, each pause a sigh,
In life's symphony, we learn to fly.
With balanced scales of joy and regret,
We face anew, no need to forget.

So let the music play on our hearts,
In the dance of life, we craft our parts.
With harmonies rich, we sing our way,
Through hope and pain, we greet the day.

Heartbeats Entwined in Lament

In the shadowed dusk, we stand,
Silent whispers wrap our hands.
A sorrowed song, a shared refrain,
Echoes of love, mingled with pain.

Lost moments flicker like a flame,
Each heartbeat calls out your name.
Yet here we are, beneath the sky,
Entwined in dreams that seem to die.

Time drifts like leaves on a stream,
Faded pages of a dreaming theme.
We dance in sorrow's soft embrace,
Eternal echoes, a fleeting trace.

But in this night, as shadows wane,
Our hearts beat on, despite the strain.
Through every tear and whispered prayer,
Lamenting love, we still declare.

The Soliloquy of Love's Antitheses

In light's bright kiss, shadows take flight,
A paradox blooms in the silent night.
Each word we speak leads to a divide,
A soliloquy where truths collide.

Your laughter dances, yet stings like frost,
In this tangled tale, what's truly lost?
Passions clash in heated debate,
With every heartbeat steeped in fate.

A hand reaching out, but drifting apart,
Opposites live in the depths of the heart.
The joy in the void, the ache in the bliss,
This is the lesson we mustn't miss.

Yet, even through the strife and the scars,
We find a beauty in our wars.
For love's game, intricate and vast,
Teaches us to hold on tight and fast.

A Tapestry of Smile-Streaked Sorrows

Threads of laughter woven with tears,
A tapestry crafted from joys and fears.
In hues of gold and shades of blue,
Each color tells a story, true.

A smile escapes, but sorrow wields,
A delicate balance, the heart yields.
We wear our masks as the world spins round,
In the fabric of life, we're tightly bound.

Moments of light, entwined with the dark,
Every heartbeat, a silent spark.
In the loom of fate, we find our grace,
Embracing the struggle, we find our place.

So here we stand, hand in hand,
In a world that sometimes feels unplanned.
Together we stitch our dreams under skies,
A tapestry vivid, where hope never dies.

The Poetry in Fading Radiance

As twilight descends and the stars ignite,
We find a beauty in the fading light.
Each whisper of dusk holds stories untold,
In the soft caress of the evening's fold.

The glow of the day may slowly recede,
But heartbeats linger, planted like seed.
In the quiet night, shadows begin to play,
Crafting memories in shades of gray.

Yet still the moon shares its tender glow,
Illuminating paths we both know.
Each moment cherished in resolute grace,
Reminds us that love embraces each space.

So here's to the dusk, the dawn yet to claim,
For in fading radiance, our hearts stay the same.
We write our sonnets on the canvas of time,
In every heartbeat, a silent rhyme.

Odes to Fleeting Moments

Time dances lightly, in whispers and sighs,
Each second a treasure, before it just flies.
A laugh shared in sunlight, a glance at the stars,
These moments, like fireflies, brighten our scars.

Evening drapes softly, the day bids goodbye,
Memories glimmer as dusk fills the sky.
In shadows we linger, yet light finds a way,
To hold onto those glimmers, not letting them stray.

In photographs captured, our smiles never fade,
Each blink of existence, a serenade.
The heartbeat of time, so fleeting, so pure,
Lingers in laughter, a bond we secure.

With every goodbye, hope flickers anew,
In the heart's quiet chambers, where dreams can imbue.
Let's gather those moments like flowers in bloom,
For life's sweetest joys are too brief to consume.

Shades of Cheer and Melancholy

A sunbeam spills laughter across a warm room,
Yet shadows still whisper of dreams that can loom.
The dance of the colors, both vibrant and grey,
Remind us of balance in life's vast array.

Joy writes in bright pigments, a canvas so wide,
Yet sorrow blends softly, it will not divide.
In echoes of laughter the heart finds its place,
While tears paint the stories that time can't erase.

Each moment a brushstroke on life's intricate page,
Where joy meets the heartache, a tender exchange.
We celebrate seasons, both light and profound,
In the tapestry woven, where wisdom is found.

Let cheer be our anchor, but melancholy's tune,
Guides us through twilight, from sun to the moon.
For in the embrace of both joy and despair,
We discover the beauty in the moments we share.

The Language of Laughter and Loss

Giggles and whispers, beneath the moon's glow,
Echoes of laughter, where warm breezes blow.
Yet shadows will linger, reminding we're frail,
In the heart of the night, silence tells a tale.

A child's innocent giggle, the sound of delight,
Wrapped in soft memories, a comforting light.
But loss paints its brush on the canvas of time,
Transforming our verses, with heart-wrenching rhyme.

We dance through the valleys of joy and of pain,
Through laughter's sweet chorus, and sorrow's refrain.
Each moment a lesson in love's vast expanse,
Uniting our souls in a delicate dance.

In laughter, we find that together we thrive,
While loss keeps us humble, reminded we're alive.
So let each note echo within us, we'll sing,
For the language of life is an intricate string.

Portraits of Happiness and Heartbreak

Smiles painted brightly, framed by our eyes,
Captured in sunlight, where hope never dies.
Yet whispers of sorrow hang heavy like air,
In the corners of pictures, where memories stare.

With every laughter shared, joy fills up the space,
But heartbreak will come, leaving only a trace.
Each moment a portrait, both radiant and torn,
Where love intertwines with a heart that feels worn.

On canvas of dreams, we create and we break,
In hues of togetherness, in colors we make.
From happiness rising like dawn's first embrace,
To heartaches that mold us, a poignant grace.

Let's cherish the snapshots of life's roller chase,
For in every heartbeat, joy and pain find their place.
In portraits of living, we pen our own art,
The story of existence, a tapestry of heart.

9 789916 907177